FEEL MY WORDS

PRATIK VYAS

"To those who carry quiet strength and unspoken dreams. May these words find you, and may you feel them as yours."

Contents

Contents

Contents

Contents

Foreword

Writing poetry has always felt like a journey inward, a search for those feelings and thoughts that lie just beneath the surface, waiting to be brought into light. After my first book, Overflow, I realized that poetry is my way of connecting myself with others who may share these unspoken moments. Feel my words is my next step along the path, a continuation of my journey to express what we often struggle to convey.

I invite you to read this book slowly, allowing each line to sit with you. Thank you for joining me on this journey; may these words become yours as much as they are mine.

Warm regards,

Pratik Vyas

Preface

Feel my words began as a simple desire to express the unspoken- a desire to bring emotions to life through words. After my first book, Overflow, I felt a pull to delve even deeper, to explore the spaces within us that we sometimes avoid. This book is the result of that journey, a collection of poems that seek to embrace and articulate feelings that lie beneath the surface, sometimes too quietly felt to be shared.

Acknowledgements

"To my family, thank you for your endless love, patience and encouragement."

1. The sky's going to fall

Returning from her place
with heavy heart and empty hands
I sit on the garden bench
with my neck leaning on the edge
as I look above
I remember the time I wasn't alone
the sky looks so close
as if it's going to fall

2. What made you?

Don't hate the people
who left you
remember the things
that once broke you
are the same things
that made you

3. Two kinds of people

• 3 •

Traveling in the rain
I saw two kinds of people
those traveling in cars
with their hand out of the window
those on bikes
looking for shelter under the bridges
for the privileged
rain is a great instagram post
for the deprived
it's one of the living cost

4. The Shelter

I walked the streets everyday
I had a home but still a homeless
I tried to stay calm but I was restless
saw someone like me one day
gazed at her with the passion of stargazer
watched her like a silent birdwatcher
she just blinked and passed by
just one look felt
like a shelter in a snowy winter

5. The daily trip

Navigating from peace to anxiety
is my daily trip
journeying towards the depth
of my thoughts
there's no turning over
cause, overthinking is my maneuver

6. My Superpower

• 6 •

I stay calm in the moments of outburst
as if staying calm is my superpower
where most lose their cool
I play it smooth
but when it comes to you
I become chaos

7. Earthen effigy

Walking across the grassland
following the trail
moving fingers over grass
eyes stuck at horizon
imagine me walking towards it
as I leave this earthen effigy

8. Keep walking

My fate has taught me
to move
getting stuck
is what it disapproves
So, be it dark
or the shining sun
I'll keep walking
if I can't run

9. Masterpiece

Your touch would make me feel
that I'm high without any drinks
like the winter breeze
caressing the skin
like the smooth strokes of brushes
creating a masterpiece

10. Cured wound

When patience blends with
destiny's will
the wound is cured and
the heart is healed

11. Trip down memory lane

Running in laps
is what I do
when I take a trip down a memory lane
going through the same moments
again and again
makes me feel me
in a world full of chaos
that makes me what I'm not.

12. Dark Clouds

Destiny laughed at me
took away the things that I needed the most
the way winds dispersed the clouds
and the loner me, longing for rain
sat there empty handed
waiting for dark clouds to form again

13. Forced Motivation

How do you accept?
the things you detest
when nothing goes right
the sorrows surround
they inflict Forced motivation
the people around

14. Let me dream

• 14 •

Make me sleep and let me dream
of the shores touching my feet
with you sitting beside holding my arm
as the sun drowning in the sea
and you curl more into me
you adore the scenic beauty in front of you
I feel that's nothing compared to you

15. Fate

Sometimes you feel you aren't destined
atrocious is the fate
god's plan, damaged
whenever you feel your hour will come
the minute hand stops at fifty nine
is it the time that stopped?
or my abandoning luck at halt

16. Broken things

Thinking of you and feeling blue
the reminiscence of the broken things
staying in memories where the distance grew
cause the heart that broke is still inside
moments to cherish, now just a few

17. Coffee brew

Went to the same place
where we first met
today it just smells of roast
without the fragrance of
your perfume made of rose
now that all the love has dried
only coffee brewed there

18. Page no. 143

• 18 •

While brushing off dust from an old book
found a photograph on page 143
in the old school photo
saw a face, little blurry
somewhere in my memory
she was the topic of the class
I was just a shy kid among the mass

19. Hurdle

My night is struck
by a harrowing grief
the light of the moon
through curtains upheld
hurting my eyes
which haven't slept well
sinking in my blanket
going down with my belief
a scent of sadness
blowing with winds
though I cheer the dark
and the silence it brings
my heart waits
for the morning spark
hurdling between day and night
hard to choose
what brings me to life

20. Love gives life

• 20 •

I went to the garden
to pluck some flowers
for my love
the plant cried-
"why you must kill someone to prove your love
love isn't supposed to take lives
it's meant to give life"

21. Lock and key

And for long he waited
waited for someone with a key
that would unlock the desires
of his own heart

22. The empty village

• 22 •

Looking for my memories
I grappled into her heart
found a place with my name written
looked like an empty village
abandoned by people

23. Dust from the past

• 23 •

So you've got some
dust from the past on your heart
blow it off
so that people can see
how beautiful you are

24. Mystery

All that misery
the heart couldn't hold
like a mystery
it is bound to unfold

25. Let's step back

• 25 •

Amidst the fear of breaking again
I tried to stop my heart's ascends
the more it tried to lean
towards the open arms
the more I warned
about those deadly charms
in those hypnotic deep eyes
you've drowned before
those whirls in the curls
have got you strangled before
the heart laughed and said
"let's just step back" for love's sake.

26. Behind the walls of oblivion

You decided to stay
behind the walls of oblivion
is it hurtful?
seeing me seeking you?
In pain and agony
I shout, punch and smite
while you sit behind,
assume everything to be alright

27. Beyond Question

Quick in the times of prosperity
slow in the times of adversity
Your strength may decline
your pace may drop
There's one thing beyond question
you have to keep moving
in spite of the scratches,
swelling and bruising

28. Losing my hope

There's no one to blame but me
for all the struggles I can't cope
I'm trying to escape this swamp
but I'm losing my hope

29. The tunnel

She was the one
who found me
under the tunnel of darkness
and gave me her light
it's okay she left
but in the same tunnel
why'd she threw me again

30. Morning light

Morning light so pure and divine
look out of the window
with your gorgeous smile
for this day is a journey towards light
go out and chase the sun
happiness would take its flight

31. Being foolish

• 31 •

Not everything is as it seems,
I'd never intend to deceive you,
how foolish could I be,
unknowingly found ways to hurt you

32. Stay with me tonight

Put your promises aside
and stay with me tonight
let me show you
the light of my heart
from inside
I will count each
passing minute
as a thousand year
I won't ask you for more
I want to live a hundred lifetimes
in this single night

33. Evergreen love

When all my efforts
to hold you
went in vain
and you still left
then I waited
I waited for so long
like a piece of desert
waiting for rain
surviving on one last hope
seeing you coming back
to me and
making my heart
bloom again
with your evergreen love

34. Curiosity killed the crow and me

Out of curiosity
I asked her his name
he was popular
she told me about all his fame
for long, in embarrassment
I did dwell
for asking question that
seemed so lame
but now it doesn't matter you see
for I have this thing within me
that forgave myself
more than her
and that is
my heart of gold
which matured well
as hardships came

35. Side by side

• 35 •

Take me on a ride
somewhere across the tides
you and me beside
somewhere on the far side
where the sea of hope
touches our dreams of the sky
let's cross it together
hand in hand, side by side

36. Confession

The day I confessed
the world fell apart
I shouldn't have told you
that I love you from my heart
now that you know
you have every right
to treat me as you like
why do I feel hurt
by the things that
never bothered me before
Is it me or you?
why I can't take it anymore?

37. The path

When I see myself here
in the middle of a dense forest
trees with roots above ground
so high that I cannot make
contact with their eyes
I walk past the gallows of sorrows
I reach the mountains of tragedies
to the valley of despair
in hopes to reach infinite sunlight
I wish I had chosen
a different path
but there wasn't much of a choice
this is how I was made
made to choose the same path
again and again

38. My solitude

Your memories haunt me
when I'm alone
but I detest those gatherings
where I just don't belong
the sarcastic chatter
that pierce my ears
the gentle banter
that turns bitter
away from those
I look for you
in my solitude

39. Pandemonium

It was only your eyes
where I could sail
into calmness
for this world is a pandemonium

40. Attention

Sometimes I can't keep up
my pace is slow
I have on and offs
my mood keeps getting low
I may commend privacy
and abstain from affection
but all I really need
is a little attention

41. Ocean of her dreams

I can't divert her flow
to nourish my barren heart
she's a vibrant river
that must unite with
the ocean of her dreams

42. Be mine

• 42 •

I had to let you go
I had to bear that pain
of seeing you with someone else
of course im happy
to see you smile
but what if your smile is
a little less that what
it could've been

43. She's not there

• 43 •

Sometimes I over do it
I keep running
towards the mirage
built from her love
even when I know
it's not there at all

44. That smile

As soon as she smiled at me
I closed my eyes
and started dreaming about us
I was on the edge
about to fall
in a pit called love
my wise past
grabbed my hand
and thank god
it pulled me back

45. It isn't worth the risk

She turns her eyes
when I return the gaze
the path to her heart
a burning maze
afraid of the outcome
her future is fixed
falling for me
isn't worth the risk

46. Your hands are tied

I know you cannot say
that you love me
you cannot hold my hand
and walk beside me
I know Your hands are tied
freedom, that you lack
bound with promises
you made long back
just look into my eyes
and say nothing
I'll just walk away
cause we can never be a thing

47. I'm tougher

Feeling helpless,
and hope is crumbling
waving at luck
my hands are shaking
though the Pain is immense
I'll bear it without a sigh
times are tough
but so am I

48. Your desire

• 48 •

Don't close your eyes
cover yourself not
I'm not the bothersome wind
or the fearful fire
but the summer's cool breeze
that your body desire

49. Would you say hi?

She may not know how I feel,
but she always knew what's best for me.
she doesn't know what I want,
but she always knew what I need.
she knows our paths are different,
so she wants to keep a safe distance.
but no paths are straight.
what if they meet again?
would you say hi or just move on again?

50. Bound to sink

The embrace has started
getting loose from her side
is there a feeling
that she's trying to hide?
she talks less now
and dull is her tone
where ships are bound to sink
I'm sailing in that zone

51. Just for you

This is why I write
I write for you
maybe someday
a random occurrence
will lead your eyes
to my words
from the eyes
my feelings will
reach your heart
and you will know for sure
that those must be my words
written only for you

52. I can handle

• 52 •

This year I spent in a dark hole
took a toll on my body and soul
optimism tells me
next year it would be gentle
wisdom advises me to prepare
for things you can't handle

53. The drift is slow

If you ever plan
to hear me out
only good things
will come from my mouth
I ain't blaming you
for anything
oh baby you and me
are still a thing
just so you know
the drift is slow
let's catch it now
make the sorrows flow

54. Ashes of love

I can still feel the smoke
rising from the letters
I burned
those words I wrote
when I was hurt
enclosed in an envelope
they never met another eye
that would shed a tear for them
all they witnessed was a blaze
and a love reduced to ashes.

55. Make it slow

It's immensely tough to
resist your glow
when I see you
the memories start to flow
your eyes has power to destroy me
I request you to make it slow

56. Fall

How tough it must be
for the trees to set free
a part of themselves
in the form of a leaf
every time they shed a leaf
I ponder the strength it takes
to let off a feeling
that survived mighty quakes
they've taught me
to stay strong
with each falling leaf
that does not belong
they've taught me
patience to wait
from season to season
until time reaches it's fate

57. I'm looking for you

• 57 •

Your memories haunt me
when I'm alone
but I detest those gatherings
where I just don't belong
the sarcastic chatter
that pierce my ears
the gentle banter
that turn bitter
away from all those
I look for you

58. Let me through

My heart wants to reach out
and express my love for you
but the wall you've built
isn't letting me through
I need you to understand
unsaid doesn't mean untrue

59. The burning moon

• 59 •

Not as bright as the sun
but the moon still burns
cursed to get torn
more and more every night
there comes a night
when it lights up the sky
with its warm light
to tell its tale
of losing itself
and growing back again

60. Preacher

They keep advising me
about the wrongs I do
but they don't realize
I'm the preacher, its true
let them cast their judgements
let them say what they will say
for i walk a path of purpose
and I'll preach another day

61. Scars

Show them your scars
they will never let them heal
keep it inside
it will burn you from within

62. Hypocrisy

I hide my flaws in the dark corners of my brain
so I can laugh at theirs, devoid of restraint
without being judged by my heart
for the hypocrisy that I keep my part

63. Autobiography

After failing to find a place
in everyone's good books
I'm planning to write
an autobiography for their
validation

64. Before you walk in my shoes

You may grow your feet
and walk in my shoes
but you'll need a big heart
to carry what i have endured

65. Silence doesn't mean agreement

I may have words
to express how sad I am
but my words would shatter
the belief that
I can't be weak
though this belief is just false
and I'm going to
lay my words down here
just so you know
my silence was not agreement
to the circumstances

66. Courage

I wish I had the courage
to acknowledge
she's not mine anymore
I cant keep asking her
for time, love, my missing needs
its her life
and that's a life without me
a life beyond me

67. Fair and just

• 67 •

Since I've become just
the world has lost its fairness
since my eyes opened to wisdom
the worlds seems inferior
Am I too hollow for them?
maybe I've lost empathy within

68. Lost days

Those deep chills that i get
as you move your fingers in different ways
now that I know how it feels
I crave for those lost days

69. My city

The city responsible for my existence,
the city that told me, "You're mine,"
and I believed it to be mine as well.
I surrendered myself to be part of it.
with a few days gone,
it denied my whole existence,
as if I were never there—
not now, not then.
even the spirit of the city,
that traveled through me,
that traveled with me,
seemed skeptical seeing me.
the living and non-living
within the city didn't even notice,
as if I were just thin air—
unseen, unfelt.
so I chose my crib
as I have accepted
that my time has passed;
the journey of life is a one-way ticket.

70. Your presence

Your dreams calm me down
when I'm feeling blue
I can only imagine
what your presence would do

71. Tiny spark

From a tiny spark
a fire ignites
through care and trust
love reaches its height

72. The evening sun

As the evening sun dipped
Into my coffee
I moved my cup
And poured the amber drink
In the memory of
The evening and the coffee

73. Forgotten

I came back to the place
I lived once
after a couple years
expecting a welcome
from the winds
that always blew over me
and I realize
I'm forgotten already

74. Temptation

Temptation called with a quiet sound
desire rose, spinning around
dreams of peace, I long to find
calm slips through my restless mind
chasing sun, with fire inside
regret splashes from guilty tides

75. Can't go back

• 75 •

90's is the time
I can never return to
fading old photographs
the past I wouldn't undo
I try to remain calm
but I'm cursed in a way
to feel the memory
that won't fade away

76. Pride

This hasn't been easy
this hasn't been simple
but I'm still proud of
the way I keep going

77. My reflection

I like to go to the lake
to see my reflection
my mirror wouldn't show
the bruises on my soul
it's only the water with ripples
that would show the real me
when life would throw stones

78. Left to sigh

You've blocked all the paths
that lead to you
you've nulled all my efforts
of seeing you
the fencing you raised
they stretch to the sky
no matter how much I leapt
I keep falling, left to sigh

79. I'd make everything right

In her fancy, sprawling city, I drove through the night
alone in the darkness, awaiting the first sunlight
whispering wind, open windows, I search for her sight
long lost love, buried deep, from that regrettable fight
I waited then, I wait still, patience stretched tight
just one more chance, I'd make everything right

80. No redemption

• 80 •

The heart broke in a blink of an eye
shattered in bits and pieces
love, trust — each was a lie
fake were the smiles and kisses
fool was I for that mocking glow
empty promises, made-up stories
how could one stoop so low?
no redemption in a thousand sorries

81. My resilient heart

• 81 •

Despite the bashing
it kept its pace
despite the breaking
it's still in the race
why wouldn't I be proud
of my resilient heart
which strived throughout
refusing to fall apart

82. I'm biased

I paint
a small layer of emotion
on my bias
to make them feel
that I'm just

83. I will survive

As soon as the distance grew
she felt empowered ignoring me
she never knew I had mastered
the art of being ignored
in shadows I learned to live
even in darkness, I survived

84. Being selfish

Your scent turned
to nothingness
in my heart
a little numbness
I could've stopped you
I could've heard you
but i lost you
to my selfishness

85. The puzzle

Like the scattered pieces of puzzle
my life was before you
piece by piece you aligned the fragments
the only thing I didn't realise
you didn't place the heart back when you left

86. Keep trying

It may be destined
but it won't come to you
if you don't even try

87. Wisdom

• 87 •

More than your future
it's your wisdom
that disapproves
of dwelling in sadness

88. This is a sign

The touch you felt
and you woke up with a smile
this is a sign
of how much I miss you
My fingers through your hair
a gentle kiss on your forehead
this is a sign
of how much I adore you
The way you hug the pillow
as if you want to cuddle more
this is a sign
that we are meeting soon

89. Day by Day

I wish to shower upon you
all the love I have
I just don't want you to
fall for me
I just don't want to
fill your heart
with all my love
just to let it drip
drop by drop
day by day
as I go away

90. Change your design

In a mixed state
I sit and think
If I was the peace and calm
that she needed
Why couldn't I be there
forever with her
for I wanted her to be
in a state of peace that she longed
Why couln't I keep her
in my arms today and forever
if it was the place
where she could relax and sigh
Why couldn't I hold her hand
until the numbness hit
if it's the only thing
I would ever want to hold
Why couldn't I keep her
in front of my eyes
cause I want to see myself
only in her eyes
Why couldn't I move my fingers
along her soft and silky cheeks
It's the only texture

that makes my senses worth and alive
If you've only planned
another realm
take me there and make her mine
grant me love and change your design

Author's Note

Thank you for joining me on this journey. Writing Feel my words has been a gift to my soul, and I hope reading it has been a meaningful experience for you. These poems are now as much yours as they are mine.

You can also check out my first book, "Overflow by Pratik Vyas", available on all major platforms.

www.ingramcontent.com/pod-product-compliance
Lightning Source LLC
Chambersburg PA
CBHW061434160726
47995CB00003B/887